Universe Books
New York

Published in the
United States of America in 1976
by Universe Books
381 Park Avenue South,
New York, N.Y. 10016

Library of Congress Catalog Card Number: 76-5091

Cloth edition: ISBN 0-87663-238-X
Paperback edition: ISBN 0-87663-947-3

Picture research by Miriam Friedman
Design by Robert Reed

Printed in the United States of America

Eight Classes of Kisses

The kiss of passion.
The parental and filial kiss.
The kiss of affection (always between women).
The devotional kiss.
The fraternal kiss.
The kiss of curiosity.
The kiss of treachery.
The fleshly, evil kiss.

—Alfred Fowler,
The Curiosities of Kissing

"Stay," he said, his right arm around her waist and her face expectantly turned to him, "shall it be the kiss pathetic, sympathetic, graphic, paragraphic, Oriental, intellectual, paroxysmal, quick and dismal, slow and unctuous, long and tedious, devotional, or what?" She said perhaps that would be the better way.

—Charles Carroll Bombaugh,
The Literature of Kissing

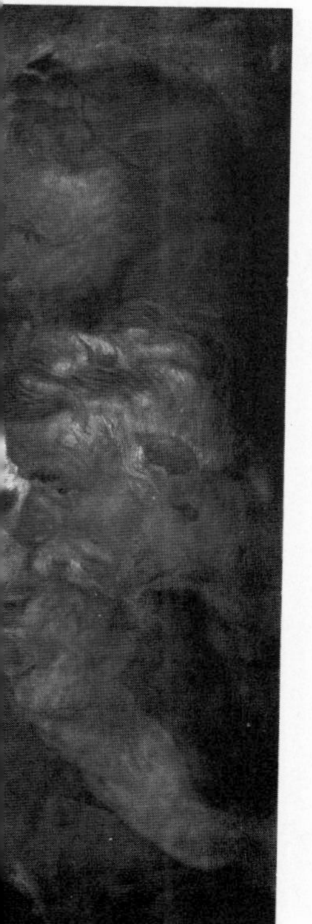

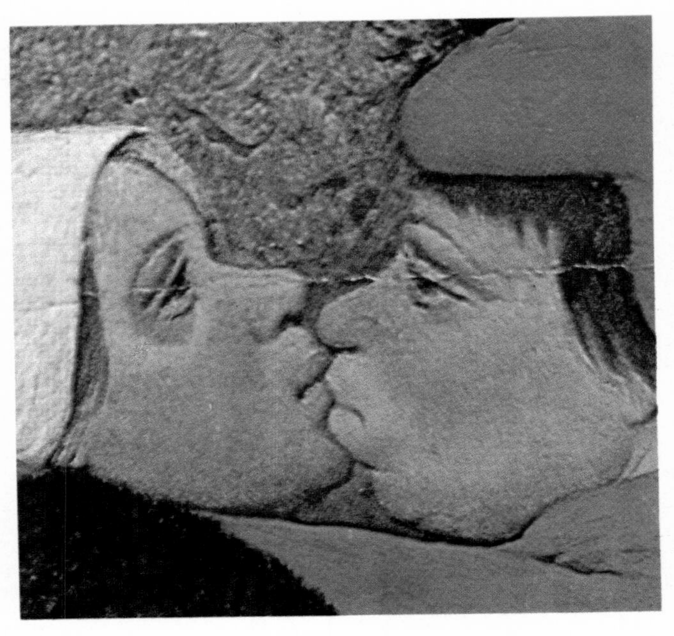

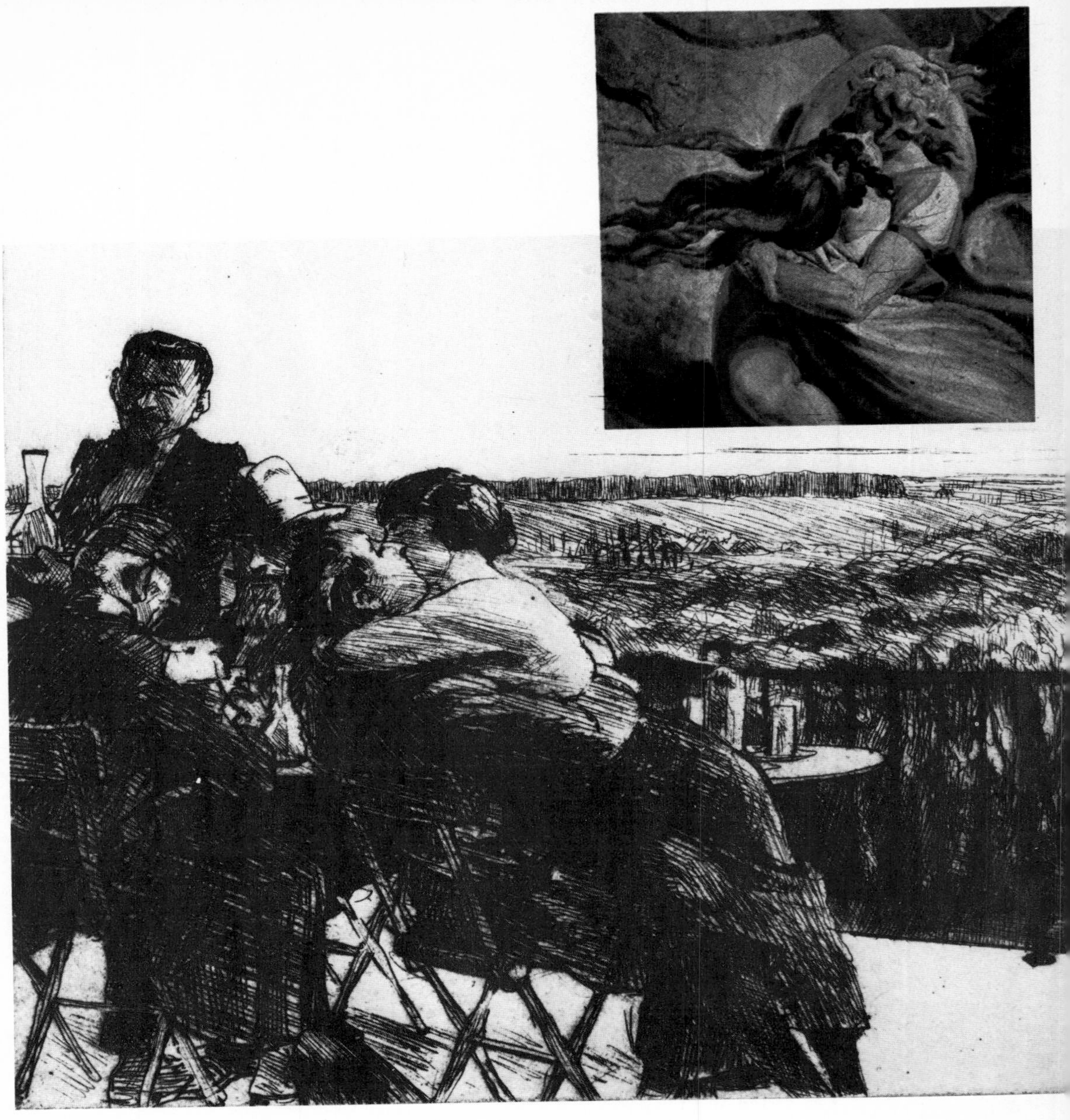

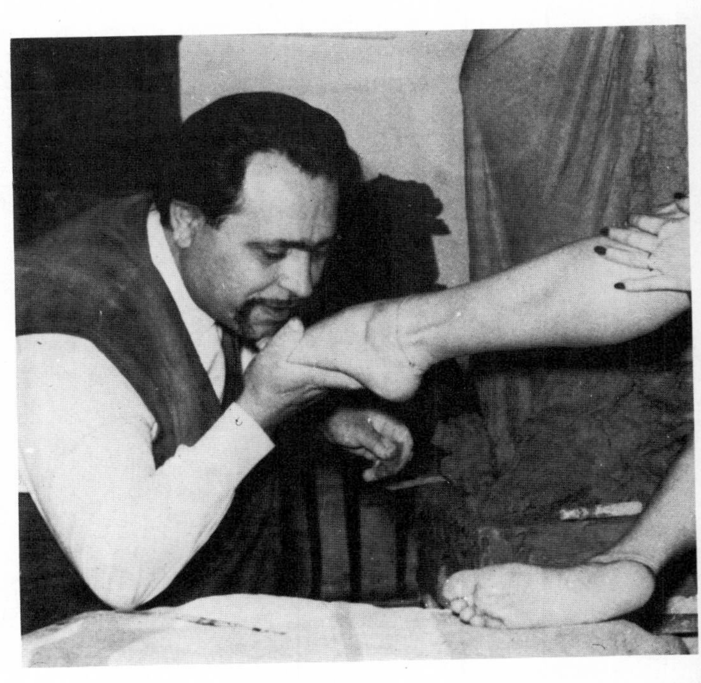

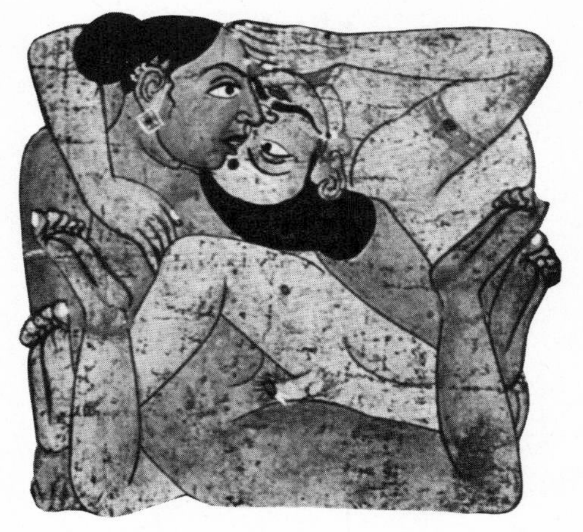

L'Amour

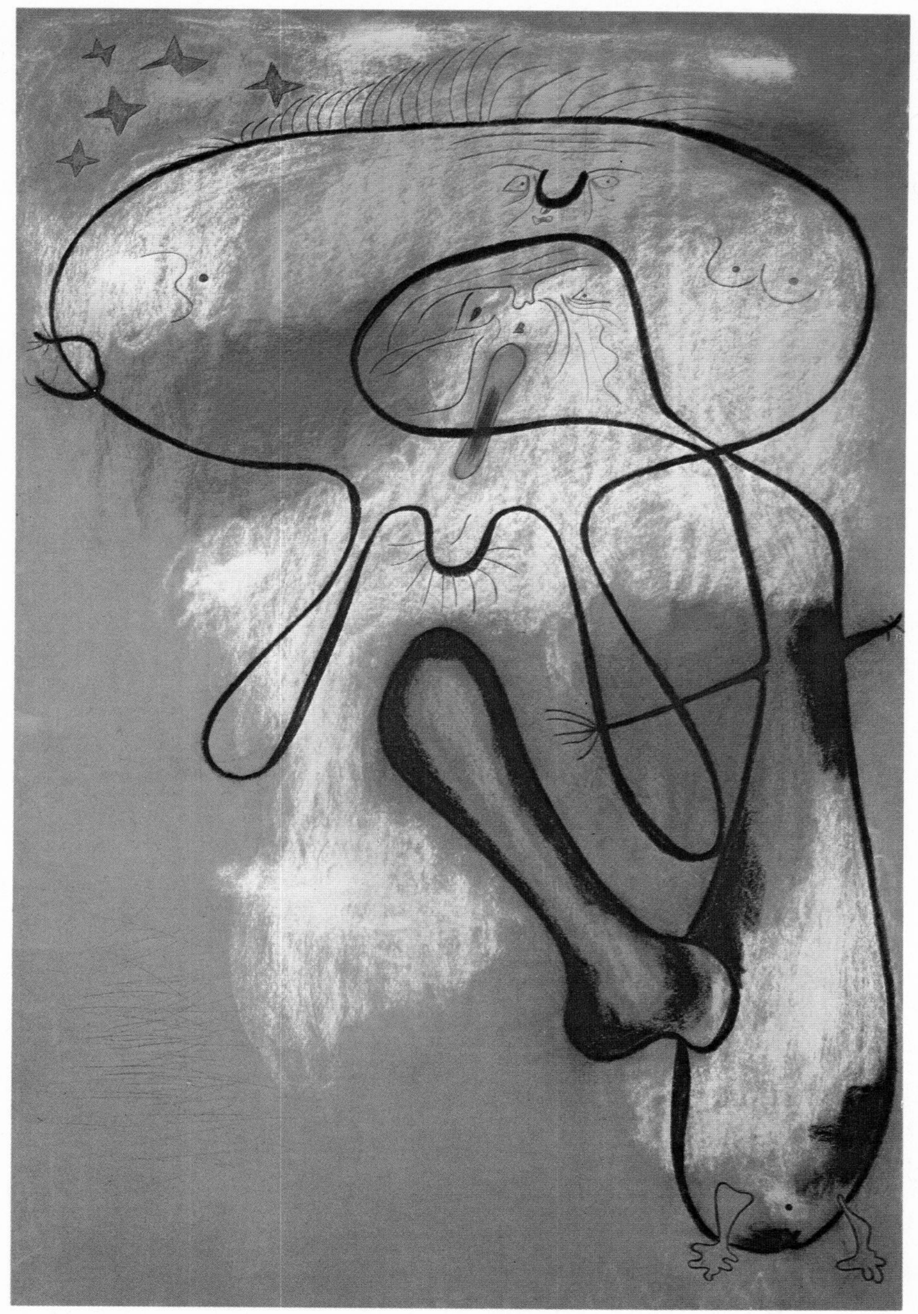

که راه دو سه روزه بیش کرد تا الختی یابد تا بخورد و پارهاء گوشت بزرگ بیکبار فرو برد و بنه خاید

واگر بیمار شود کبی بخورد نیک شود و چون زخمی خورد از تیر و مانند و دندانش بماند طلب شعد کند و بخورد

تا از آن او بیرون آید و آلات اندرونی شیر جمله با آلات اندرونی سگ ماند در آفرینش و از خروش شیر شنید

و موش بترسد و کاروانی که در و خروش شنید باشد بر نشان گزند نکند و از هیچ جانور نگریزد که از نور حه

و پادشاهی موجه بر شیر جانست که پادشاهی بشه بر پیل و بوزکا و میش از ناله و بانگ شیر تا ...ت

DOWN IN JUNGLE TOWN,
A HONEYMOON IS COMING SOON,
THEN YOU'LL HEAR A SERENADE
TO A PRETTY MONKEY MAID,
AND IN MONKEY LAND
THE CHIMPANZEES SING IN THE TREES
"SHE'LL BE TRUE TO MONKEY DOODLE-DO"
WAY DOWN IN JUNGLE TOWN.
WORDS BY
MUSIC BY

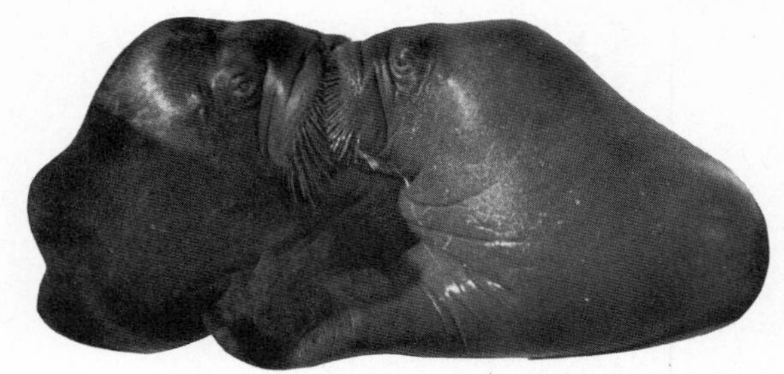

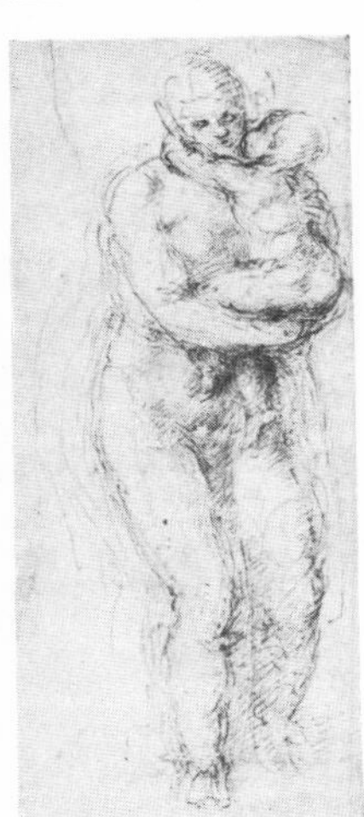

LA STRAGE DEGLI INNOCENTI
ORATORIO DI DON LORENZO PEROSI

AND DOES BABY GET A NEW FUR COAT?
SHE'S KIND TO 'DUMB ANIMALS'

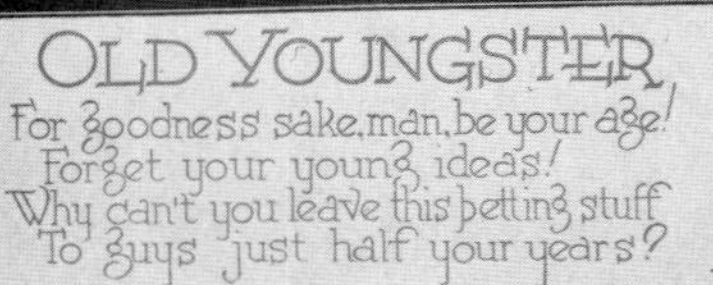
OLD YOUNGSTER
For goodness sake, man, be your age!
Forget your young ideas!
Why can't you leave this petting stuff
To guys just half your years?

LA GRANDE
FOLIE
FOLIES BERGERE

Reine de Joie
par
Victor Joze
tous les
libraires

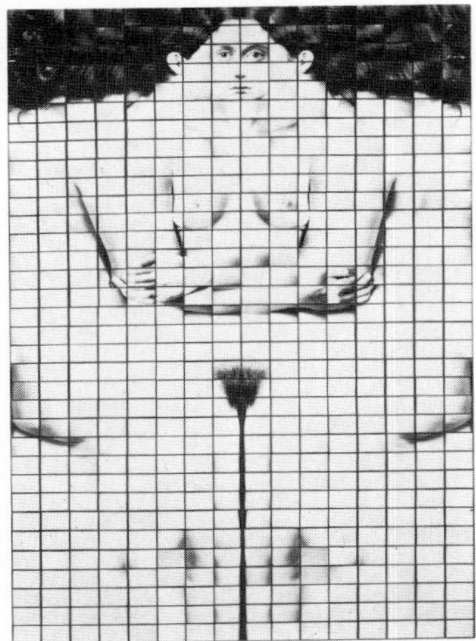

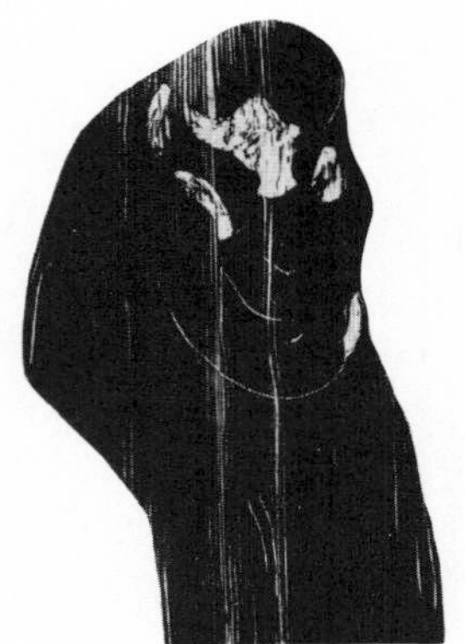

THINK

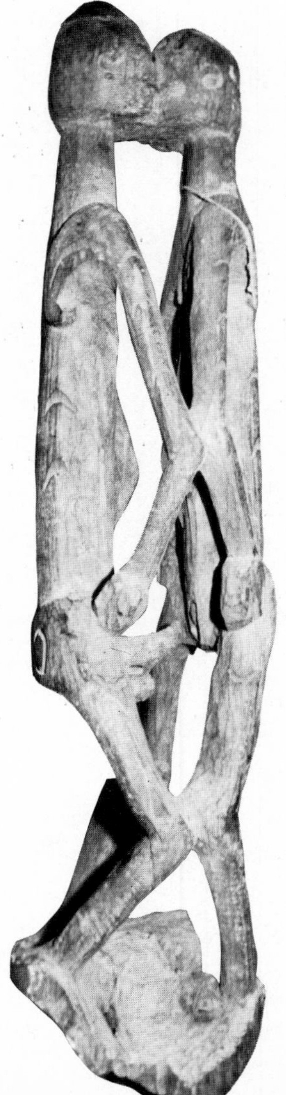

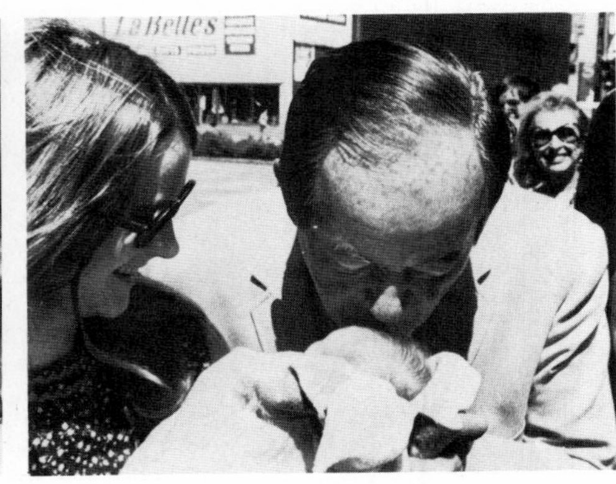
LaBelles

THE UNITED

L'Amour
en Sous Marin
VISE PARIS
2280/2

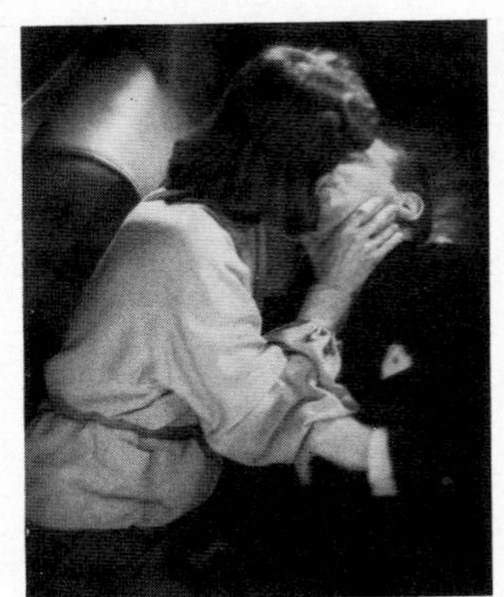

YOU SHOULD COME
TO MEET ME MORE OFTEN.--

YOU ARE
MUCH SWEETER
THAN THE
SWEETEST
BLOSSOMS.

WHAT WOULD YOU SAY,
IF I WOULD TELL YOU,
THAT I LOVE YOU ?--

Behind this maiden stealthily across
the flower strewn lands,
Her lover comes and over her eyes
he clasps his loving hands
"Now maiden tell me who it is that
holds you thus so fast"
He whispers, but she will not speak
until his hands unclasp.

She starts and blushes crimson as he
takes his hands away,
Then laughing happily she gives to
him her sweet bouquet.
"Ah, loved one, Take these flowers so fair,
I plucked them all for you; they are
fresh and fragrant
And still moist with last night's starry dew."

He stoops and kisses her red lips He
looks deep in her eye-
He whispers. "Fairest flower of all,
I'll love you till I die
For with the flowers you give to me,
I take your heart so true,
And it is far the fairest flower,
that in loves garden grew."

THE LADIES' HOME JOURNAL
THE MAGAZINE WITH A MILLION
FEBRUARY
1904
TEN
CENTS
HIS VALENTINE

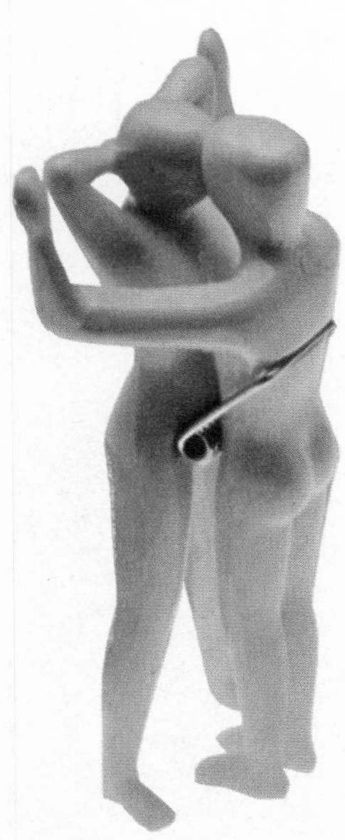

The sound of a kiss is not so loud as that of a cannon, but its echo lasts a great deal longer.

—Oliver Wendell Holmes

List of Illustrations

25. Etching, Pablo Picasso. © SPADEM, Paris, 1976.

26. Shunga woodcut, Suzuki Harunobu, mid-18th century.

27. Shunga woodcut, Kitagawa Utamaru, late 19th century.

28. Gouache, Nepal, 18th century. Collection, Ajit Mookerjee, London.

Gouache, Kangra, c. 1800. Collection, Ajit Mookerjee, London.

29. LOVE MAKING, Raoul Dufy, woodcut, 1912. Collection, The Museum of Modern Art, New York; purchase fund.

30. EROTIC GROUP, terracotta, c. late 2d century B.C. Delos Museum. Photograph courtesy of the Institute for Sex Research, Inc., Bloomington, Indiana.

31. THE LOVERS, Joan Miró, pastel, 1934. Philadelphia Museum of Art; the Louise and Walter Arensberg Collection. Photograph by Alfred J. Wyatt.

32. Detail from a Greek water pot, late 6th century B.C. Kunsthistorisches Museum, Vienna.

SATURN AND PHILYRA, Guilio Bonasone, engraving. The Metropolitan Museum of Art, New York; the Elisha Whittelsey Fund, 1959.

33. TAUROMACHY I, Pablo Picasso, etching, 1934. Collection, The Museum of Modern Art, New York; acquired through the Lillie P. Bliss Bequest.

34. THE KISS, Will Bradley, poster, 1896. Photograph courtesy of Scala New York/Florence.

TITANIA, BOTTOM, AND THE FAIRIES, Henry Fuseli, oil, 1793-94. Kunsthaus, Zurich.

35. Illumination from a Persian manuscript, Maragha, 1298. The Pierpont Morgan Library, New York.

36. Sheet music cover, 1908.

Photographs by United Press International.

37. Photograph by Ian Berry/Magnum.

38. ADORATION OF THE SHEPHERDS (detail), Giulio Romano, oil. Photograph courtesy of Scala New York/Florence.

39. VIRGIN WITH THE CHRIST CHILD AND ST. JOHN BAPTIST (detail), Bernardo Luini.

40. Photograph by United Press International.

41. Photograph by United Press International.

42. MOTHER AND CHILD, drawing, Ben Shahn, 1953. © Estate of Ben Shahn.

ROMAN CHARITY, Jules Lefebvre, Salon of 1894. Melun Museum, Melun, France.

THE VIRGIN AND CHILD, Michelangelo, drawing, c. 1560 ©Trustees of the British Museum.

43. Theater poster. Photograph courtesy of Scala New York/Florence.

44. THE ENTHRONED VIRGIN MARY, Quinten Massys.

THE PAZZI MADONNA, Donatello, 1420-22.

45. ESKIMO MOTHER AND CHILD, photograph by Richard Harrington.

46. Detail of the altarpiece of Selmecbanya, Hungary, c. 1506.

Princess Margaret and Queen Elizabeth, photograph by United Press International.

THE TWO LOVERS, Jean-Honoré Fragonard, oil. Collection, Leopold Rey. Photograph courtesy of André Held, Ecublens.

47. FRIENDS, Gustav Klimt, 1904-7. Osterreichische Galerie, Vienna.

Pat Nixon and Mamie Eisenhower, photograph by United Press International.

48. Print.

President Truman and Archbishop Athenagoras, photograph by United Press International.

Tony Janiro and Rocky Graziano, photograph by United Press International.

49. BROTHERS, Ben Shahn, tempera, 1946. Hirshhorn Museum and Sculpture Garden, Smithsonian Institution, Washington, D.C.

50. American valentine.

LIKE TURTLE DOVES, George Grosz, watercolor. Courtesy of the Estate of George Grosz, Princeton, N.J.

51. Poster, Pico, prior to 1928.

QUEEN OF JOY, Henri de Toulouse-Lautrec, poster lithograph, 1892.

52. THE STOLEN KISS, Jean-Honoré Fragonard, oil, c. 1766.

THE LOVERS, Giulio Romano (?), oil, 1540.

53. CARDINAL AND NUN, Egon Schiele, oil, 1912. Collection, Dr. Rudolf Leopold, Vienna.

54. THE DILIGENT MAID AND THE DISSOLUTE MAID, etching, 1796.

55. Woodcut, Le Campion.

56. WINTER, Tetsu Okuhara, photo-collage, 1971. Collection, The Museum of Modern Art, New York.

THE KISS, Peter Behrens, woodcut, 1898. Collection, The Museum of Modern Art, New York; gift of Peter H. Deitsch.

57. TWIN HEADS, Alfred H. Maurer, oil, c. 1930. Collection of Whitney Museum of American Art; gift of Mr. and Mrs. Hudson D. Walker (and exchange).

58. PIETA (detail), Sandro Botticelli, tempera, 1500. Museum Poldi-Pezzoli, Milan.

59. THE LOVERS, René Magritte, oil, 1928. Collection, Richard S. Zeisler, New York, N.Y.

60. HECTOR AND ANDROMACHE, Giorgio de Chirico, oil, 1917. Collection, Gianni Mattioli, Milan.

THINK, William N. Copley, oil, 1964. Collection, The Museum of Modern Art, New York; gift of Miss Jeanne Reynal.

THE KISS, Edvard Munch, woodcut, 1898, Munch Museum, Oslo.

61. YOU-ME, Ay-O, serigraph, 1976. Nantenshi Gallery, Tokyo.

62. DEATH SEIZING A WOMAN, Kathe Kollwitz, lithograph, 1934. Collection, The Museum of Modern Art, New York; purchase.

DEATH AND THE MAIDEN, Edvard Munch, drypoint, 1894. Munch Museum, Oslo.

63. KISS OF DEATH, Edvard Munch, lithograph, 1899.

64. JUDAS, Ben Shahn, drawing, 1964. © Estate of Ben Shahn.

65. Mithuna couple, stone, 12th-13th century. The Metropolitan Museum of Art, New York; purchase, 1970, bequest of Florence Waterbury.

Asmat carving. Photograph courtesy of Weidenfeld & Nicolson. © Christine Harrisson.

67. THE KISS, Constantin Brancusi, limestone, c. 1912. Philadelphia Museum of Art; the Louise and Walter Arensberg collection.

CLOTHESPIN, Claes Oldenburg, corten steel, 1976. Centre Square, Philadelphia. Photograph, by Neil Benson, courtesy of Jack L. Wolgin, Philadelphia.

68. ETERNAL SPRINGTIME, Auguste Rodin, plaster, c. 1884. The Rodin Museum, Philadelphia.

69. PASSION, Gaston Lachaise, bronze,

1932-34. Lachaise Foundation; courtesy of Robert Schoelkopf Gallery.

70. Soldier kissing Western Wall in Jerusalem, photograph by Gilles Caron. Courtesy of Liaison Agency, New York.

72. DESCENT FROM THE CROSS, Pietro Lorenzetti, fresco. Lower Church of S. Francesco, Assisi. Photograph courtesy of Editions d'Art Albert Skira, Geneva.

74. Fidel Castro and Hubert H. Humphrey, photographs by United Press International.

75. Gerald Ford and Charles DeGaulle, photographs by United Press International.

76. GOOD-BYE IN THE MORNING, L.P. Debucourt, engraving, 18th century.

THE RETURN, A. Deveria, lithograph, 19th century.

COUPLES, photograph by Ernst Haas/Magnum.

77. THE MEETING AT THE GOLDEN GATE, Giotto, fresco. Scrovegni Chapel, Padua.

78. THE KISSING COUPLE, photograph by Robert Doisneau. Courtesy of Rapho/Photo Researchers, New York.

79. THE GANG, photograph by Bruce Davidson/Magnum.

80. A CHRISTMAS FREEBOOTER, R. Caton Woodville, drawing.

81. WINTER, George Barbier, calendar illustration, 1925.

82. French postcard.

83. Photograph by United Press International.

WE ROSE UP SLOWLY, Roy Lichtenstein, oil and acrylic, 1964. Hessisches Landesmuseum, Darmstadt, Germany; Karl Stroher Collection. Photograph courtesy of Leo Castelli, New York.

84. Photographs by United Press International.

85. FLYING PUTTO KISSING ANOTHER PUTTO, Antonio Allegri Correggio, fresco, early 16th century. S. Giovanni Evangelista, Parma.

86. Greta Garbo and Melvyn Douglas in *Ninotchka*. From NINOTCHKA, edited by Richard J. Anobile, a "Film Classics Library" title which recreates this famous motion picture by means of more than 1,500 frame blow-ups and complete dialogue. © 1975 Darien House, Inc. Published by Universe Books and Avon Books, and in England by Jupiter Books and LSP Books.

87. Photograph by United Press International.

Shirley MacLaine and Robert Mitchum in *What a Way to Go*.

88. Postcards from the collection of Carol Wald, New York.

89. Postcards from the collection of Carol Wald, New York.

90. "Courting Couple" courtesy of the General Research and Humanities Division, The New York Public Library, Astor, Lenox and Tilden Foundations.

French postcard.

German postcard

91. French postcard.

92. COUPLE, photograph by Miriam Friedman.

93. Magazine cover from the collection of Carol Wald, New York.

From advertisement by Nikasinovich for Guerlain lipstick and nail polish. Courtesy of Guerlain S.A., Paris.

94. NEIGHBOURLY REFRESHMENT, lithograph.

95. KISS ME QUICK, lithograph, Currier & Ives.

96. X-RATED PAPER CLIP. Photograph courtesy of Bloomingdale's, New York.